Eleanor Allen

Wartime Children 1939-1945

Adam and Charles Black · London

Collecting metal salvage

Black's Junior Reference Books

General Editor: R. J. Unstead

1	Houses	R J Unstead
2	Fish and the sea	Spike Noel
3	Travel by road	R J Unstead
4	The story of aircraft	Robert J Hoare
6	Mining coal	John Davey
7	The story of the theatre	David Male
8	Stars and space	Patrick Moore
9	Monasteries	R J Unstead
10	Travel by sea	Robert J Hoare
12	Musical instruments	Denys Darlow
13	Arms and armour	Frederick Wilkinson
14	Farming in Britain	Frank Huggett
15	Law and order	John Dumpleton
16	Bicycles	Frederick Alderson
17	Heraldry	Rosemary Manning
18	Costume	Phillis Cunnington
19	The story of the post	Robert Page
21	Castles	R J Unstead
23	Coins and tokens	Philip Leighton
24	Fairs and circuses	Paul White
25	Victorian children	Eleanor Allen
26	Food and cooking	Margaret Baker
27	Wartime children 1939–1945	Eleanor Allen
28	When the West was wild	Robert J Hoare
29	Wash and brush up	Eleanor Allen
31	Canal people	A J Pierce
32	The story of oil	Roger Piper
33	Home sweet home	Eleanor Allen
34	Outdoor games	Frederick Alderson
35	Horses	Fiona Somerset Fry
36	Earthquakes and volcanoes	Sara Steel
37	Going to school	Alistair Ross

Published by A & C Black (Publishers) Limited,
35 Bedford Row, London WC1R 4JH

ISBN 0-7136-1503-6

Filmset and printed in Great Britain by BAS Printers Limited Over Wallop, Hampshire

Contents

1 Introduction 5
2 The sights of war 6
3 Gas masks 8
4 Evacuation 10
5 Air raids and shelters 16
6 Black-out 23
7 The threat of invasion 25
8 How children helped 26
9 Food rationing 28
10 Babies 34
11 Clothes rationing 35
12 Other shortages 38
13 Dig for victory 39
14 Schools 42
15 Pets 47
16 Toys 48
17 Sport 51
18 Radio and films 52
19 Travel 55
20 Holidays 57
21 Effects on family life 58
22 Victory celebrations 61
Some more books 63
Index 64

A London school is evacuated

Hitler will send
no warning –
so always carry
your gas mask

ISSUED BY THE MINISTRY OF HOME SECURITY

Some evacuees only had plimsolls and no proper shoes.
The cardboard boxes contained their gasmasks

The author and publishers are grateful to the following for permission to reproduce photographs:

Barton Transport Ltd 56a, b; BBC 52b, 53b; Daily Herald 52a; Fox photos 47b, 48a, 49a; Fyffes Group Ltd 30a; Crown Copyright: Imperial War Museum 4a, 5a, 7c, 8a, b, 10a, 12a, 15, 16a, b, 18, 20b, 22b, 23a, 25a, 26a, 28a, b, 29b, 30b, 31a, b, 33, 34d, 35a, 38a, b, 39a, 40, 41a, b, 42a, 4ba, 46, 47a, 49b, 55a, 57a, 58a, 63; Mansell Collection 37b, 42b; Radio Times Hulton Picture Library 1, 2, 3, 4b, 5b, 6a, b, 7a, b, 9, 10b, c, 11, 12b, 13, 14, 17a, b, 19a, b, 20a, 21, 22a, 23b, c, 24a, b, 25b, 26b, 27a, 29a, 32, 34b, 35b, 36a, 37a, 38c, 39b, 43, 44, 45b, 50a, b, 51a, 54, 55b, 57b, 58b, 59a, b, 60, 61a, b, 62; Surrey County Cricket Club 51b; PF White 48b.

1 Introduction

At 11.15 am on Sunday 3rd September 1939 the British Prime Minister, Mr Chamberlain, made a special radio broadcast to the nation from the Cabinet Room of 10 Downing Street. He announced that from 11 am that morning a 'state of war' had existed between Britain and Germany.

Families sat by their radio in stunned silence as the Prime Minister made his announcement and called upon everyone to help in defeating the German leader Adolf Hitler. It was a great blow to them. Many adults could remember only too well the horror of the First World War which they had fought little more than 20 years before. After the settlement of that war they had hoped for a lasting peace, but now the world was plunging into a great war a second time.

Though most people felt Britain was in the right and were determined to win the war, they thought of the stresses that Chamberlain had warned would lie ahead. Even for those not fighting, there would be hard work, suffering, and danger. Parents looked anxiously at their children and wondered how best to protect them.

But to the children themselves the announcement of war meant very little. Immediately after hearing it they were rushing outside to play.

'Adolf Hitler is Victory !'—A Nazi propaganda poster

A Nazi rally, with Hitler taking the salute

5

2 The Sights of War

War brought many changes to all aspects of life in Britain, but perhaps the changes that children noticed first were the ones they could see around them in the streets.

In towns the appearance of shops changed. Suddenly their plate-glass windows were covered with long strips of sticky tape, sometimes arranged in patterns. This was known as window strapping. If a shop was struck by a bomb the glass would not fly out and injure passers-by; it would crack, but the tape would hold the pieces in place.

Bus and train windows were even more carefully strapped. They had a fine net pasted over them. Much to the children's annoyance, this stopped them seeing out.

In the streets of major towns there were huge piles of sand bags protecting important buildings from bomb damage. Sand bags were also used to protect air-raid wardens' posts. The warden himself, riding a bicycle in his navy blue uniform, was another familiar sight on the streets of wartime Britain.

Children who lived near factories watched them being camouflaged with grey, brown and green paint so that from the air the buildings merged into their surroundings.

Shop windows strapped so that the glass would not fly out if the shop was struck by a bomb

A barrage balloon (left) and sandbags outside a public shelter

Hanging low in the sky overhead were large, silver-grey, whale-like objects. These were hydrogen-filled barrage balloons. The balloons were controlled from parks or waste land by men from RAF Balloon Command, using steel wires.

At night children watched as great searchlights swept across the dark sky, practising for the time when their beams would pick out an enemy plane and make it a clear target for the ack-ack (anti-aircraft) guns.

Open spaces were also used as sites for emergency water tanks. These large, open tanks of water were used when bombing had wrecked the main water supply. Firemen fighting the blazes caused by bombs drew their water from these emergency supplies. The tanks were fine places to play. Despite repeated warnings, some children fell in and were drowned.

Everywhere one went there were men and women in uniform. On the roads there were convoys of hundreds of lorries, full of soldiers on the move. There were not only British forces, but also American, Free French, Polish and Commonwealth troops. Boys enjoyed comparing the different uniforms and equipment.

3 Gas Masks

1. Hold your breath. Put on mask wherever you are. Close window.

The Germans had used poisonous gas as a weapon in the trenches during the First World War. Now there was a fear that they might use it again, this time dropping it over Britain from their bombers.

The Government supplied each person with a rubber gas mask and they painted the tops of pillar boxes with a special yellow gas-detector paint.

People were supposed to carry their mask around with them because there would be little warning of a gas attack and no time to dash home. At first, places of entertainment such as cinemas would not let people in unless they were carrying a mask.

Regular gas drills were held at school. At a signal from the teacher all the children had to stop work and put on their masks as fast as possible. The teacher timed them. Sometimes classes spent the whole morning or afternoon working in their masks to get accustomed to them. They did not enjoy that, because the masks had a powerful rubbery smell and the mica window at the front tended to steam up.

The baby helmet worked, but mothers and nurses hated it. Most babies howled when they were placed inside and it was very bulky to carry around. If the mother stopped pumping in air, the baby would suffocate even if there was no gas

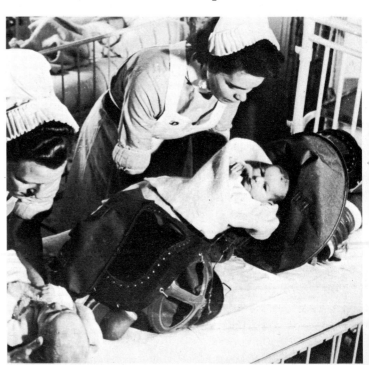

Children found it hard to take these practices seriously, especially after they had discovered that they could blow raspberries through the rubber. One girl remembers having what she claims could have been a fatal attack of the giggles when another girl pretended to blow her nose at the end of her mask.

The Government thought that young children might be afraid of gas masks, so they had a special Mickey Mouse gas mask designed for under-fives. It was brightly coloured in red and blue. Children laughed at the funny faces and enjoyed putting them on.

There was a problem about what to do for babies who obviously could not use the ordinary sort of mask. This was solved just before the outbreak of war by the invention of the baby helmet.

As the war dragged on, people began to lose their fear of gas attack. A fresh scare came in 1944, but that too came to nothing. Much to everyone's relief, the gas masks and gas drills never had to be used.

Air-raid practice at a girls' boarding school

4 Evacuation

For more than a million children who lived in large industrial cities and major ports throughout the British Isles, the outbreak of war meant a separation from their home and family. These children lived in the areas most likely to suffer heavy bombing, so the Government urged their parents to send them to the country where they would be safe. Some children returned home after only a few weeks or months, but others stayed in their country foster homes for the whole six years of the war.

Those who were lucky enough to have relatives or friends in the safe areas went to live with them, but most children were evacuated by the government. Very young children went away with their mothers, but children of school age usually went together as a school.

It must have been a very sad moment for both parents and children when the time came to say goodbye. Many of the children had never been away from home before—now they were going perhaps a hundred miles away to live among strangers.

The children lined up in the school playground wearing special armbands or labels for identification. Each carried a gas mask case over his shoulder, and a small suitcase or bag containing clothes. Teachers and special helpers marched the children down to the bus or railway station and travelled with them.

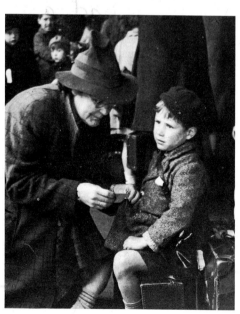

Labelled for the journey, just like a parcel

Sometimes the journey was very long and exhausting, and not even the teachers knew where they would end up. Each child was given a stamped postcard to send home to let his anxious parents know where he was.

Billeting officers had gone round homes in safe areas to list the ones that had room to take children. Normally, as the children arrived they were driven off by the billeting officers in ones and twos and deposited at their billet. In some areas, however, local people went to the station to meet the evacuees and pick the ones they wanted.

This was not a very good way of finding homes for children. The nicely dressed or pretty children were chosen first and it was very upsetting for the few who were left until last.

There were frequent mix-ups. A whole school would arrive in a town where they were not expected, or perhaps find another school had taken over quarters meant for them. When that happened they spent a weary night wrapped in borrowed blankets on the floor of a church hall until matters could be sorted out in the morning

Bathtime for an evacuee family

A village school. Notice the wire mesh over the windows and the gas mask cases

Many of the evacuated children came from poor homes in overcrowded areas of large cities. But the country people who had a room to spare were often those with a large house and a high standard of living. Hosts were horrified to find that some children had no stouter footwear than a pair of plimsolls and had brought no change of clothing with them. They had to go out and buy pyjamas and underwear for the children, paying out of their own pocket.

Some of the children were found to have head lice or skin diseases. This was hardly surprising because before the war few families in cities had bathrooms. Soon hosts were complaining.

Sometimes the situation was reversed and children found that their billets lacked many of the comforts they had known at home.

The evacuees were often very nervous and unhappy in their strange new surroundings. They missed the friendly bustle of a large family, city cinemas and fish and chip shops, as well as some of their old friends.

But despite the difficulties, many children settled down well with their foster parents. They grew so attached to their new home that they cried bitterly when they had to leave it. Often they kept in touch through letters and visits for years afterwards.

Teachers who went with their school tried to make sure that the children's work went on as normal. This was not easy because some schools found themselves working in village halls without proper equipment, or sharing the premises of the local school on a shift system. While the local school used the classrooms, the evacuees would have games on the playing fields or go for nature rambles.

Local children did not always get on well with the newcomers, referring to them as 'the invading hordes', or 'the vackees' and blaming them for any damage that was done.

Teachers had to sort out the problems of children who were unhappy in their billets and generally be like parents to them. It must have been a great strain on the teachers. One girl remembers that out of the staff evacuated with her girls' school, 'One committed suicide, one died of a heart attack, and one had a nervous breakdown, all within the space of a year.'

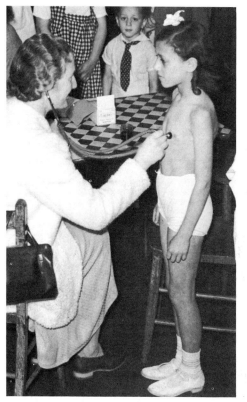

Parents tried to visit their children whenever they could, but some found the journey long and expensive. They began to miss the children and to worry about them. If the children themselves began to show signs of homesickness, it was tempting to fetch them home. As the months went by, the heavy bombing the government had forecast did not come.

People began to doubt the bombing ever would be as bad as the Government had feared, and wondered if there was any point in leaving the children in the country. When the Government decided that parents should pay a sum of money each week towards the support of their evacuated children, many felt they could not afford it. More and more parents started to fetch back their children. All through the autumn there was a steady trickle home. Finally Christmas arrived and the children went home to celebrate. Once home, the majority did not return.

Later in the war there was a further spell of evacuation caused by the attacks of pilotless planes and rockets, but on the whole the scheme had fizzled out.

Sea-vacuation

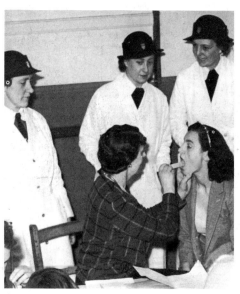

Medicals for sea-vacuation

In 1940 there was a great fear that Britain would be invaded and parents were anxious about what would happen to their children in the chaos that would follow. The Government announced a scheme for sending children to safety overseas. Countries such as America, Canada, Australia and New Zealand offered hospitality to Europe's children.

The idea was very popular and applications poured in to the Children's Overseas Reception Board. Thousands of children remained abroad for the five years of the war, forming lifelong friendships.

The scheme was not without tragedy, however. One ship carrying children was struck by a torpedo or mine in the Atlantic. Many were drowned, but 46 survived after floating in a lifeboat for eight days.

Posters like this urged parents not to give way to the temptation to bring children home, but thousands did

5 Air Raids and Shelters

In the First World War people had been caught unprepared by air raids from zeppelins and bombers. In the Second World War Britain expected air attack and was ready.

As soon as war with Germany seemed a possibility, volunteers began to train as ARP (Air Raid Precaution) wardens. They learned how to cope with air raids and care for casualties. When enemy planes crossed the coast, a warning siren would sound—a wailing note which rose and fell. One long, continuous note gave the 'all clear'—the raid was over.

Every home received a leaflet explaining how to prepare for such emergencies as a fire bomb falling through the roof. People were advised to keep buckets of sand handy to extinguish fires, and to keep a bath or tank full of water. One nervous old couple filled up their bath obediently, and then kept it filled with the same water until it turned green and slimy.

'I was never allowed to bath there,' remembers their unfortunate lodger.

A direct hit

Clambering into the Anderson

Anderson or Garden Shelters

In 1939 the Government began to deliver air-raid shelters to the areas most likely to be attacked. The garden shelter was the most common type of family shelter, but it was never very popular.

If the siren sounded in the middle of the night, people hated having to leave their warm bed and snatch up their sleeping children to dash outside into the garden. The shelter was cold and damp and they had to huddle together in their warmest outdoor clothes. Frightened families sat in the dim candle light listening for the drone of enemy planes overhead.

The 'all clear' siren was a great relief to everyone. 'We sprang out into the garden like so many jumping crackers,' says one child. The other great drawback of the garden shelter was that it often filled up with water. Some families had regular baling-out sessions; others had to abandon theirs as useless. 'We had a frog swimming in ours,' a woman complained.

Parents sang, read or told stories to distract the children and tried not to let them see how afraid they were themselves

The Morrison shelter could be used as an ordinary table, as a table-tennis table, or even as a playpen

The Morrison or table shelter

Because people were so reluctant to go outside to use the Anderson, the Government introduced a new type of shelter which could be set up in the living room. It looked like a large steel table. At night two adults and two children could sleep comfortably in it, though one boy remembers seven visiting relations crowding in. The Morrison was not so strong as the Anderson, but it was more popular—raids seemed less scaring in the familiar surroundings of the living room.

Not everyone had a home shelter. Some people strengthened their cellar with wooden props and used that. In fairly safe areas the outer wall of a room was strengthened with sandbags. Other people, even if they had a shelter, preferred to dash into the cupboard under the stairs!

Surface shelters and tubes

Communal shelters were built in densely popu-lated areas. They had poor ventilation and when they were crowded the atmosphere became very thick. But for a time they were popular. Families went along there every night to sleep and enjoy the companionship of other families. But soon it was discovered that they could become death traps because they could not withstand a direct hit.

Then London people began to use the tube stations instead of the surface shelters. Each night thousands carried down bedding and slept on the platforms. At first there were inadequate toilet facilities and poor lighting, but later these were improved. People sang and talked together to keep up their spirits. Lonely people enjoyed going there for company.

Communal shelters at Peckham

Entertainment in the London Tube

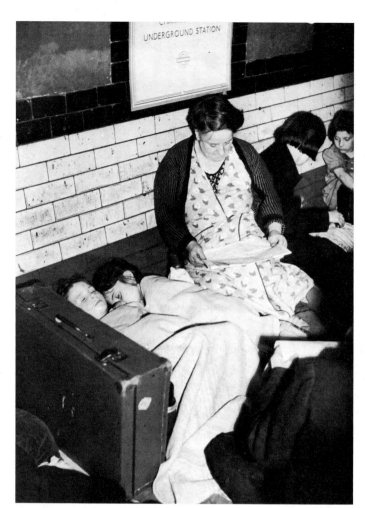

Sleeping in the Tube (left) and survivors from an air-raid coming out of their Anderson shelter

The worst raids of the war were known as the London Blitz. They began in September 1940 and carried on until May 1941. Large areas, particularly in the East End, were flattened. Thousands of people were killed and thousands more were injured or lost their homes.

The populations of large industrial towns such as Coventry suffered too, and so did those in large sea ports such as Bristol, Liverpool and Hull. In what became known as the 'Baedeker Raids' (after the famous Baedeker guidebooks for tourists) Hitler tried to destroy towns with important historic buildings such as Bath and Canterbury.

Towards the end of the war a new terror came to the people of London and the South East. Pilotless planes called V1s (nicknamed buzz bombs or doodle bugs because of the noise they made) were sent over from German bases in France. When they ran out of fuel they crashed to earth.

People listened to hear the engine cut out, which it did with a loud roar. If it cut out immediately overhead they flung themselves to the ground or under a table. The V1s were followed by rockets called V2s which crashed without any warning at all.

Waiting to collect hot water at the street corner when the gas and electricity were out of action

This Plymouth market carried on despite the destruction all around

More than 60 000 men, women and children were killed in Britain by air raids; thousands were seriously injured. Whole town centres such as Coventry's were flattened and schools, shops and houses were wrecked. Reception centres were opened for families who had lost their home and all their possessions.

The air raids were a nerve-racking experience, but most children seem to have withstood them remarkably well.

Incendiary bombs were dropped to start fires

6 Black-out

The black-out was one of the inconveniences of war shared by everyone. It meant blacking out all lights after dark to confuse enemy aircraft in their night bombing raids on densely populated areas.

When daylight faded, the world out of doors turned pitch black—no street lights, no neon signs, not even a friendly chink of light from a house. At first, regulations against showing a light were so strict that people got into trouble for lighting a cigarette in the street. Later, when regulations were not quite so strict, people could use a torch, provided it was dimmed with two layers of tissue paper. Cars could use their headlights too, if they were shaded.

To make sure no light shone from their home, families bought thick black cloth to hang at the windows, or used sheets of black paper fixed to strips of wood which fitted into the window frame. Sometimes only the windows of main rooms were blacked out; in bedrooms people undressed in the dark.

"Some day I really will try waiting for a few minutes to get used to the blackout... ..... if only I'm still here"

ISSUED IN SUPPORT OF THE MINISTRY OF WAR TRANSPORT'S ROAD SAFETY CAMPAIGN BY THE TILLING GROUP OF COMPANIES

The Warden made sure that no chinks of light were showing

Decorated blackout curtains in a hospital

In the first month of blackout, the number of people killed in road accidents nearly doubled. White lines were painted along kerbs and men were advised to leave their shirt tails hanging out at night

People tried to avoid going out on very dark nights. 'We did all our visiting and entertaining on moonlight nights,' one woman remembers. Those who did venture out often had difficulty making their way home, like this girl:

'I remember coming home from a relative's house nearby with my mother. It had turned foggy and in the combination of fog and blackout we got hopelessly lost in a few yards. It was more frightening than any air-raid!'

To guide fumbling keys in the dark some householders painted the key hole with luminous paint. Local authorities painted white lines along kerbs, gateposts, treetrunks and steps as a guide, and all car owners had to paint the running boards and bumpers of their vehicles white.

Despite the paint precautions there were still many injuries as a result of the black-out. People collided with each other, tripped over sand bags or fell down flights of steps. Some, to their embarrassment, found themselves apologising to lamp posts.

7 The Threat of Invasion

When the Germans invaded France in 1940 everybody expected the next move would be the invasion of Britain. The Government warned people to be prepared.

'Do not give the German anything. Do not tell him anything. Hide your food and your bicycles. Hide your maps. See that the enemy gets no petrol. Think always of your country before yourself.'

Sign-posts and mile-stones were pulled up and the names of railway stations and any other signs giving the name of a place were painted out to confuse the Germans and slow up their advance. The Home Guard was formed to fight the invader and reserve dumps of food were distributed to every town and village because there would be a breakdown in normal life. Some people had their own secret dump of tinned stuff buried in the garden.

The signal that the invasion had started was to be the ringing of church bells, so of course they were banned for other uses. 'If the church bells rang during school hours we were supposed not to panic but to leave the children at school,' remembers a mother, 'but I did not know any mother who was prepared to do that.'

There were many false alarms, but in fact the invasion never came and Britain was spared the dreadful experience of being occupied by the enemy.

Don't forget that walls have ears!

CARELESS TALK COSTS LIVES

Signs were painted out or removed in the hope of confusing the enemy

8 How Children Helped

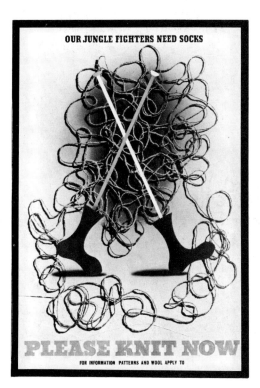

OUR JUNGLE FIGHTERS NEED SOCKS

PLEASE KNIT NOW

FOR INFORMATION PATTERNS AND WOOL APPLY TO

Children of all ages were encouraged to feel they could help the war effort. Boys aged 16 to 18 could join the Air Training Corps which was started by the Air Ministry. Later they could join the Sea Cadets or the Army Cadets instead. These organisations were very popular, partly because they gave boys the opportunity to wear a uniform.

Girls joined the Girls' Training Corps or Women's Junior Air Corps, both of which gave them training in first aid, drill and signalling.

Those who did not wish to join a military organisation could give help through the Scout or Guide movement. Scouts filled sandbags and firebuckets or tested stirrup pumps, whilst guides did useful work in hospitals or made collections.

For boys under 18 there was work to be done in the Communication or Messenger Service. They ran messages for the forces or the Home Guard.

'Cogs' find a bath and other metal salvage in a village

Younger children joined the 'Cogs' which was the name given to junior salvage collectors. Their job was to search out from neighbours' waste and rubbish anything that could be useful as salvage. Scrap metal such as cooking utensils, tins, or ornaments could be melted down and used again as parts for aircraft. Waste paper, rags, bones, jam jars and bottles were other useful items the Cogs eagerly rescued from dustbins.

Children who did not belong to a group could still help the war effort through their school. Schools made collections of books and jigsaw puzzles which they sent to the forces. Some schools 'adopted' a particular ship or platoon and held raffles to provide comforts for them.

Girls avidly knitted socks, mittens and balaclava helmets for troops or prisoners of war, thinking as they did so of the brave men their efforts would help to keep warm. 'I felt guilty for years,' a girl confessed, 'because I was given oiled wool to knit stockings for sailors and never got them finished.'

9 Food Rationing

WASTE THE FOOD
AND
HELP THE HUN

Britain relies a great deal on imports. Only part of the food we eat is actually grown or produced here. Most of it is carried to our ports in large refrigerated cargo ships from overseas.

During the war it was not easy to import goods into Britain for three main reasons. First, cargo ships ran the grave danger of being sunk by torpedoes, bombs or mines. Secondly, some of the countries from which we usually buy goods were occupied by the enemy. Thirdly, even if cargoes reached Britain safely there was still the danger they would be destroyed in the warehouses by air attacks on ports.

As the war continued, less and less food reached Britain's shops. There was still enough to go round, but only just. If some people were greedy and bought more than they really needed, others would be left without.

In this difficult situation the Government decided that the fairest thing was to introduce a system of rationing so that nobody, no matter how rich or greedy, could buy more food than anyone else.

'There is enough for all if we share,' they said. 'Rationing is the way to get fair shares.'

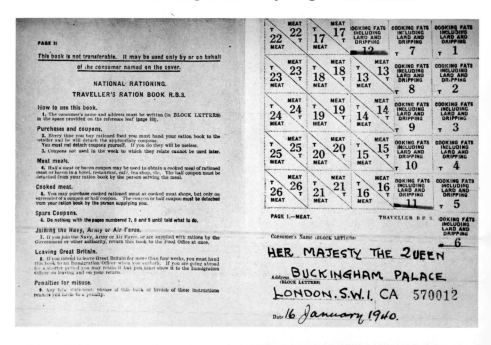

From 1940 onwards there was a shortage of basic foods such as meat, sugar, butter, eggs and cheese. Because these foods are so vital to health the Government decided to allow each person a definite weekly ration of each. Amounts varied, but an average weekly ration for each person was 1s 6d worth of meat, 8 oz sugar, 4 oz butter or fat, 1 egg, 1 oz cheese.

Tea was also put on a weekly ration of 2 oz. To make the ration last, people were advised to use 'one spoonful each and none for the pot.'

Less vital foodstuffs were also in short supply. Eventually the Government decided to ration those too, but on a different system. Rice, jam, biscuits, dried fruit and tinned stuffs were each given a points value and each person had 20 points a month to use on whichever of these foods he wanted most.

Food on points rationing could be bought from any shop, but the weekly ration of basic foods could only be bought from one shop where the person was registered as a customer.

Everyone had his own ration book containing the points. The baby had a green book, the children blue, and the adults a buff one. Usually mother took charge of all the family's ration books and had the difficult job of working out how many points to spend on various items.

Shopping took more time because many assistants left to do war work. People had to learn to queue patiently

Some foods such as oranges and onions were rarely seen in the shops. When there was a supply of oranges they were usually reserved for children under five and expectant mothers. Bananas disappeared altogether. When they reappeared after the war they were a mystery to many children. Some children didn't realise they had to be peeled and had a very unpleasant first bite!

One little girl is said to have eaten her first banana on a train, just as it went into a tunnel. In an anxious voice she asked her little brother;

'Have you eaten your banana yet?'
'No.'
'Well don't,' she warned. 'It makes you blind.'

Fresh fish was not rationed, but it was hard to find. From time to time rather odd types of fish appeared on the fishmonger's slab—tuna, whale-meat chopped into steaks, and a tropical fish with the unappetising name 'snook'.

Substitutes were introduced for certain scarce foods. Saccharine tablets were used for sweetening in place of sugar, and margarine was used instead of butter. Some foods were sold in powdered form, such as milk, potatoes and eggs. The Ministry of Food gave careful instructions about how to turn powdered eggs into successful scrambled eggs and other dishes, but people often complained that the results tasted like foam rubber.

I'm an Energy Food!

Says 'POTATO PETE'

A NEW FISH DISH

FRESH-SALTED COD

9D lb.

A clear plate means A clear conscience

Don't take more than you can eat

The sale of white bread was prohibited because it did not contain enough vitamins. It was replaced by 'National wholewheat bread'. Despite the Government's claim that it was better, many people said it gave them indigestion.

Because there was only one small helping of meat for each meal there was usually something filling to make it go further. Vegetables were fairly plentiful and appeared on the table done in all sorts of different ways—stuffed, turned into pies, in a stew, as rissoles, or as a pudding. 'Marmite' was a favourite ingredient for flavouring such dishes.

People ate a lot of tinned meat such as 'spam' sent from America and tinned fish, usually pilchards. Tinned salmon was a very rare luxury. Some shopkeepers were accused of keeping it 'under the counter' for favourite customers.

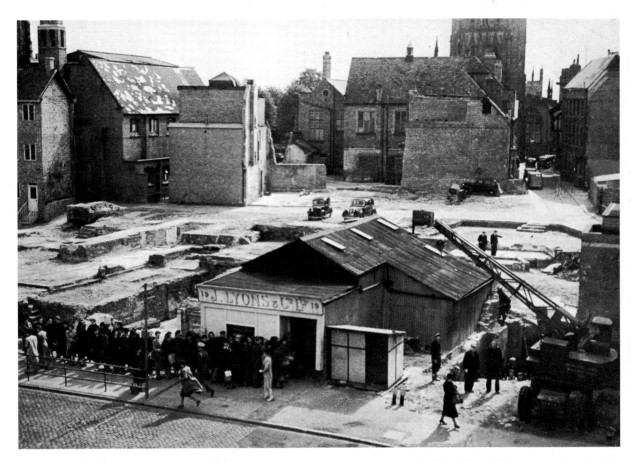

A temporary Lyons cafe put up in the centre of Coventry

Entertaining was difficult with some foods in such short supply and other foods rationed. Guests who came to stay were expected to hand over their ration books.

Children continued to have parties, but they involved careful planning and concocting by mothers. One boy became very wary of parties because, he said, 'you never knew what people were going to try out on you.'

Wartime icecream was made with soya flour. 'Banana spread' was really mashed, cooked parsnips with banana flavouring. One girl still remembers with embarrassment how her mother's concocted icing for her ninth birthday cake turned out so rubbery the children couldn't eat it.

People usually managed to have the traditional pudding and cake at Christmas, either by saving up dried fruit for months in advance or by using substitutes such as grated carrot, grated apple and chopped prunes.

Sweet rationing

For children, this was one of the greatest hardships of the war. In 1942 the Government announced a ration of 8 oz of sweets or chocolate per person every four weeks (the equivalent of one chocolate bar a week).

Many mothers were rather pleased about it. They knew their children's teeth would be healthier without sticky sweets to rot them.

Perhaps one consolation for children was that wartime chocolate was not so nice to eat. It was dark and rather coarse. 'Blended' (a mixture of milk and plain) was nicer, but scarcer. Well known varieties such as Mars bars were almost unobtainable.

The Ministry of Food and women's magazines tried to help by suggesting recipes for making sweets at home. Toffee seems to have turned out quite successfully made with golden syrup, cocoa, sugar, and dried milk.

British airmen draw their sweet rations. American servicemen were known to have large supplies of sweets, and soft hearts. Wherever they went they were pestered by hordes of children shouting 'Got any gum, chum?'

10 Babies

The Government was anxious that the health of babies and pregnant mothers should not suffer as a result of food rationing, so they introduced the Welfare Foods Scheme. Through this scheme mothers and babies received a special supply of blackcurrant juice, cod liver oil and (later) orange juice, as well as extra milk, meat, eggs and fresh oranges when they were available. Because of this scheme many mothers and babies were better fed during the war than they had been in peacetime.

There was also an extra allowance of clothing coupons for providing the baby's clothes and nappies, but finding a pram and cot was often difficult. Parents either advertised for second hand ones or bought the Government's 'utility' versions. Mothers did not like these much because they were very plain and looked, they claimed, like a box on wheels. Some mothers did not buy a cot at all, but used a drawer from a chest of drawers instead.

A home for evacuees under the age of five, whose mothers could not be with them

11 Clothes Rationing

The raw materials and the workers in clothing factories were wanted by the Government for war work, such as making uniforms for the forces. By putting clothes on ration they limited the number people could buy, and therefore limited the number of civilian clothes that would have to be made.

People were given clothing coupons similar to the ones already used for food. A 'coupon value' ticket was pinned to each item of clothing as well as a price ticket so that shoppers could work out if they had enough coupons as well as enough money to buy it. Each person had an average of 48 coupons a year to spend on whatever items of clothing he needed most.

If you look at the list on the right, and work out how many new items of clothing you usually have in a year you will realise how many they had to go without.

Points needed for children's clothing

mackintosh 7 (10, if lined)
jacket or blazer 6 (8, if lined)
cardigan or sweater 5
trousers (woollen) 6
dress 5
gym tunic 4
shirt 4
pyjamas 6
underpants or knickers 2
shoes, football or hockey boots 2
socks or stockings 1

Using a clothes ration book at Woolworth's

A clothing exchange where children's outgrown clothing could be swopped for larger clothes

Children were measured at school and those who were big for their age and were outgrowing their clothes rapidly were given extra coupons. Often parents used their own coupons on the children, but it was still impossible to buy the children all the new clothes they needed.

'Make do and mend' became the new slogan. Newspapers, magazines and Government pamphlets gave mothers advice on how to make the family's clothes last longer by careful washing and mending. 'Remember,' they said, 'a stitch in time saves not only extra work in the end, but precious coupons.'

Mothers learned how to mend frayed collars and cuffs, darn woollies, or hide a worn elbow with a fancy patch. 'I had a fawn coloured cardigan,' a girl remembers. 'Every time it needed darning it was done in a different bright coloured wool in stars and daisies until eventually it was the gayest garment imaginable.'

People did not waste old clothes. If father's old trousers were cut up carefully they could be turned into a pair of shorts for his son and a skirt for his daughter. Girls unpicked old woollens and reknitted the wool into a different pattern. The Women's Voluntary Service organised clothing exchanges where children's outgrown clothing could be swapped for larger items. Outgrown wellington boots were very much in demand as swaps because they were no longer being manufactured.

Sometimes clothes were made out of rather unusual materials. A girl in her early teens was delighted to receive a nightdress made from a nylon parachute as a Christmas present from a friend.

Boys probably didn't mind having to make do and mend as much as girls did, though one boy claims his chief memory of life in the war is having to wear patched trousers!

12 Other Shortages

WANTED

FOR SABOTAGE

THE SQUANDERBUG *ALIAS* **HITLER'S PAL**
KNOWN TO BE AT LARGE IN CERTAIN PARTS OF THE KINGDOM
USUALLY FOUND IN THE COMPANY OF USELESS ARTICLES, HAS A TEMPTING LEER AND A FLATTERING MANNER
WANTED
ALSO FOR THE CRIME OF 'SHOPPERS DISEASE'
INFORMATION CONCERNING THIS PEST SHOULD BE REPORTED TO

Many miners had joined the forces or were working in factories, so less coal was produced. Families were asked to save fuel by heating only one room, eating more cold meals, and switching the light on only when necessary. It was forbidden to use more than five inches of water when having a bath. A line was painted round the bath to indicate the correct level.

A shortage of workers and raw materials in other industries meant it was difficult to buy a large variety of goods such as razor blades, toiletries, torches, saucepans—even beer. 'Don't you know there's a war on?' was the shopkeeper's usual response to disappointed customers.

Some unscrupulous traders managed by one form of wangling or another to obtain goods that were either scarce or rationed. They illegally offered these to people for a high price and made large profits. This was known as 'black-market' trading. To buy or sell black-market goods was very unfair.

'All honest people realise that trying to beat the ration is the same as trying to cheat the nation,' said the Government and black-market traders were severely dealt with.

If **every** bone, however small, is salvaged the ships now bringing bones to this country can be released to carry munitions.

save every bone

Petrol coupons

13 Dig for Victory

This was the slogan used by the Ministry of Agriculture to encourage people to grow as much food as they could here in Britain to make up for the shortage of imported food.

'No garden is too small to help feed the family next winter,' the Ministry said. 'Flowers and lawns won't help.'

Fired with enthusiasm, people dug up their lawns for potato patches and planted vegetables and fruit trees in their flower beds. Some schools made part of their grounds into gardens where the children worked in their breaks and dinner hour. Even in parks the colourful flower displays were ousted in favour of dreary rows of beans, cabbages, or carrots.

'A few hours weekly in the garden or allotment is the duty of every able-bodied man, woman and child,' urged the Ministry.

With the help of newspaper hints, radio talks and government leaflets many families who had never before grown fruit and vegetables had the pleasure of eating their own produce, as well as the satisfaction of feeling they were helping their country.

Clapham Common turned into allotments, March 1940

Another way in which people could help make up for the shortage of food was by keeping livestock. Families who had never owned more than a pet goldfish boldly joined the war effort by keeping pigs, rabbits or ducks. Clubs were started where owners could discuss their problems and the RSPCA issued leaflets on animal care. Some schools started to keep livestock which the children learned to look after.

Dustbins labelled PIG SWILL appeared on street corners to collect household scraps for feeding the neighbourhood pigs. Hens were fed on scraps and peelings mixed with 'balancer meal'. To obtain the meal a family had to forfeit their egg ration, so it was very important that the hens should lay. To celebrate the momentous laying of their hens' first egg one family placed it on a union jack and floodlit it with a reading lamp!

Of course families often became fond of their livestock and treated them as pets. When the time came to kill them for the pot there were wet eyes among the more tender-hearted members of the family. One girl remembers going without Christmas dinner because the family were eating their own ducks.

By 1943 many farm workers had been called up and farmers were short-handed. The Government urged people to 'Lend a hand on the land' and schools asked for volunteers. Harvest camps were set up where children could live in tents for a couple of weeks whilst helping on nearby farms. They did such jobs as stooking corn, weeding, picking fruit or digging up potatoes, often working with landgirls or prisoners of war.

It was hard work. Unfortunately some farmers were scornful about the children's efforts. 'I was done in after pitchforking twenty sheaves,' one boy remembers, 'so I wasn't all that useful.'

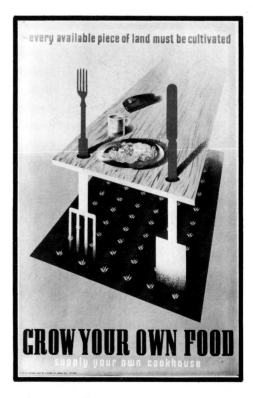

14 Schools

For those not affected by evacuation, the war still brought many problems—crowded classrooms, untrained teachers, constant interruptions to lessons, and grave shortages in supplies of stock and apparatus. No less than one school building in five was damaged by bombs and had to be closed for a time or completely rebuilt. Other schools were taken over as headquarters for Civil Defence services.

Pupils who suddenly found their school closed either had to go without teaching or attend other schools. If they attended elsewhere they created serious overcrowding. The numbers in classes increased to 60 or even 70, which made life very difficult for both pupils and teachers. 'It had to be mass teaching and rigid discipline,' says a master.

Children who did not join another school roamed the streets and often got themselves into trouble.

A primary school classroom

Air-raid drill at the Whelley Central Elementary School, Wigan

Apart from a shortage of school buildings there was also a shortage of teachers because many of the men had joined the forces. To fill the gap, they brought in elderly people, those not healthy enough to fight, and conscientious objectors.

The elderly teachers tended to be rather old-fashioned in their methods, or had eccentric habits which made them unpopular with their pupils. Boys' schools were worse hit than girls', so that many boys had to be taught by women for the first time.

Pupils also suffered from interruptions in the daily routine of the school. There were gas mask drills and air-raid practices—'a bit like fire drills nowadays and not taken any more seriously by the pupils.'

Air-raid shelters were built in the playground or on the playing field. When there were genuine alerts the children had to make their way into the shelter as quickly as possible, or they were sent home if they lived nearby. They took books to read in the shelter or sang songs such as 'Ten Green Bottles' or 'One Man Went To Mow'.

Trying to work in gasmasks

For some children the alert was a welcome interruption if it happened in an unpopular lesson, but for older children taking important examinations such as School Certificate (which has been replaced by GCE) the air-raid warning caused a major disruption.

A girl at school in Chichester remembers her class being sent into the shelter on their honour not to discuss the exam paper. They could hear gunfire from Dunkirk at the time. She claims they did not discuss the paper, but feels they must have been marked very generously because of the circumstances.

In some areas schools were temporarily closed at the height of the air-raids and lessons were held in pupils' homes, usually on two mornings or afternoons a week. A group of about eight pupils met together and the teacher who visited them left a lot of homework. The system was not very successful. Many pupils probably reacted like this boy:

'It was a novelty at first, but then it became boring because we realised we were not learning very much.'

There was a cut-back in the supplies of stock sent to schools. Paper was in short supply. Pupils' exercise books were regularly inspected to make sure that no space was being wasted, and the usual rules about good lay-out with margins and a line missed under headings were abandoned—every inch of space was used.

Practical subjects were badly hit. There was a shortage of wood for woodwork. 'Any piece of wood we got our hands on we treated with great reverence,' says a boy. 'Also the teacher set a tremendously high standard to slow up our progress so we didn't get through too much work, and precious wood.'

In needlework girls learned how to make-do-and-mend, turning old dresses into blouses. In domestic science they learned such wartime economies as making sponge cake without fat and using dried egg.

A savings drive organised by a school

There were constant reminders of the war. Most classrooms had a large map on which pupils could follow the progress of the fighting as the teacher explained it to them from news bulletins. There were savings drives, raffles, and knitting sessions for the forces. Sometimes teachers who had joined up paid a visit in uniform. The deaths of old boys, some with brothers or sisters still at school, were read out in morning assembly.

About one in three children started to stay for school dinner because their mothers were doing war work in factories, and all children received a third of a pint of milk each day to make up for shortages at home.

Despite all this, the war did not dominate the children's school life. They saw it merely as a background to the smaller, more personal happenings of school and home. Last night's unfinished maths homework loomed larger than the threat of German invasion.

15 Pets

Feeding animals was a problem because food was just as short for them as for humans. Horsemeat intended for dogs and cats had to be sprayed with green dye, otherwise unscrupulous traders tried to pass it off for human consumption.

Some pets turned to crime to supplement their diet, stealing their owner's meagre ration of meat, or raiding the butcher's shop when his back was turned. The tub of pig swill on street corners was reckoned fair game by the dogs and cats of the area and it is doubtful how much of it ever reached the pigs!

Some pets seem to have adapted well to wartime conditions. Cats and dogs often learnt to recognise the air-raid siren and beat the rest of the family in the dash to the shelter. Some people owed their lives to their pets. These animals led rescue parties to where their owners lay, buried under bomb debris, and for this they were awarded a specially inscribed collar.

The war brought extra work for the RSPCA which opened animal rescue centres for animals bombed out of their homes. Inspectors went to the scene of every air-raid to rescue any pets they could and put others out of their misery. They used a long stick with a loop at the end called a 'Dog and Cat Grasper' to pull them from the debris.

Rabbits can be fed on:

Hedgerow Weeds	Garden Waste	Kitchen Scraps
Hedge Parsley	Brussels Sprout Stems	Pot Scrapings
Plantain	Lettuce Leaves	Table Scraps
Sow Thistle	Cabbage Leaves	Root Peelings
Dandelion	Waste Potatoes	Fish Waste
Groundsel	Lawn Mowings	Pea Pods

Red Cross dogs, specially trained to lead rescue parties to people buried in bomb debris

16 Toys and Games

Toys tended to become propaganda, as with these costumes

In the first two years of war there was no great shortage of toys. Many military toys appeared in the shops—imitation sten guns, rifles, helmets and boxes of soldiers. But gradually they disappeared as the factories, workers and materials were all given over to war needs. Then there was an acute shortage of toys.

When a birthday or Christmas was approaching parents had a difficult time trying to find suitable presents. Some parents advertised for second-hand toys, or if they were skilful enough, tried making them. They ransacked the family ragbag for old scraps of material to make rag dolls or cuddly animals for younger children, and used filling from an old cushion or laddered stockings as stuffing.

Some fathers were able to carve simple wooden toys. Anyone who was skilled at making toys had no shortage of buyers and could ask a high price.

A boat made out of wood from a crashed plane; the sails were made from an old christening robe

Left: Hero worship at Aldershot
Right: A war museum

Many children set up a 'war museum' in their home and competed with each other in hunting for prize exhibits. Propaganda leaflets dropped from German planes, uniform badges and buttons, bomb fragments, and long strips of silver paper dropped to interfere with radar tracking systems were popular exhibits. But the real 'prizes' were pieces of shot-down aircraft—nosecaps, fins, or parts of the instrument panel.

'A Nazi plane was shot down near us on the Downs', recalls one child. 'I don't know what happened to the pilot, but before the police got there to guard it we children had stripped it bare. I remember thinking how frail it was. We had marvellous fun climbing in and out of it.'

Sometimes children found unexploded bombs and proudly reported them to the police. This was very exciting for the children, but worrying for their parents who were always afraid they might blow themselves up. Some did.

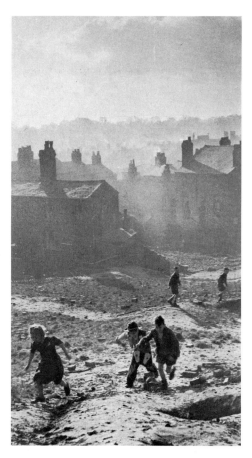

Bomb sites made first-class places to play

Both boys and girls became keen aircraft spotters. They eagerly bought books on the subject or exchanged the latest copy of a magazine called *Aircraft Spotter*. The British planes, such as Spitfires, Hawker Hurricanes and Wellington bombers were fairly easy to spot. There was much more prestige in having spotted a German plane—a Junker, Heinkel or Messerschmitt—before being hauled into the shelter.

Bomb sites made exciting play areas where children could clamber among the rubble or cautiously explore the empty rooms. Spy scares led to the invention of 'spy games' when innocent acquaintances or passers-by were tracked and watched for suspicious movements.

Cycling was a popular pastime because petrol rationing kept traffic off the roads. Long expeditions were made into the countryside along virtually empty roads. For children who were evacuated from towns the countryside itself provided an endless source of interest and pleasure.

'Toys and games were not important to me,' one boy remembers. 'It was too much fun living in the country for the first time.'

17 Sport

All forms of sport were badly hit by the war. From 1939 onwards professional football leagues were reorganised on a regional basis to save travelling time for the teams. Crowds at the matches were restricted at first to $\frac{1}{8}$ and later to $\frac{1}{4}$ of the ground's capacity because of the disaster that might occur if a crowded ground were bombed. Air raid warnings often interrupted play.

The young, fit, professional players were immediately recruited into the forces and to replace them clubs had to employ youths or part-time players from industry or the forces. One boy who was a keen supporter of Aston Villa commented on the number of bald heads in the war-time team!

There were some cricket matches between forces teams, but there was no county championship. Many sports grounds were bombed or taken over for war needs. The Oval, for instance, became a prisoner of war camp. The Rugby Union ground at Twickenham was given over to Civil Defence.

Gad, sir, Lord Sportingsquirt is right. It's only fair we should give the Germans a good start this war. After all, we won last time, y'know.

RETURN MATCH by **BLIMP**

The Oval cricket ground in use as a prisoner-of-war camp

18 Radio and Films

WHAT A WAR!
by Gilbert Wilkinson

"Stop making the kitten purr, I can't hear a damn thing!"

Both radio and the cinema held a very important place in children's lives during the war. Nowadays they are simply two out of many forms of entertainment offered each evening. Then they were the only two of importance. There were no youth clubs or discotheques, no out-of-school activities; there was no playing out after dark because of the black-out, and perhaps most important, no television.

In their own homes families either made their own entertainment or they listened to the radio. Just as certain television personalities and programmes become very popular with the family these days, so certain radio personalities and programmes did then.

Every evening younger children tuned in to 'Children's Hour' to listen to *Larry the Lamb's Adventures in Toy Town*. It was introduced by Uncle Mac who had an assistant called David. At the end of each programme children listened to Uncle Mac's parting words, which were the same each evening: 'Goodnight children—everywhere.'

Uncle Mac broadcasts from a zoo

Young people evacuated to New York taking part in a two-way Christmas broadcast

Later in the evening children were allowed to sit up and listen to *ITMA* (It's That Man Again). This was probably the most popular programme of the war years, full of odd characters and catch phrases which everybody took up.

Children listened to most radio programmes if they were allowed to, but their other favourites were likely to be comedy programmes such as 'Hi Gang', patriotic talks by J B Priestley, programmes of popular music with the singer Vera Lynn, and the national anthems of allied nations played on Sundays.

Of course families always listened to the news, as this girl remembers. 'My father always switched on for the news. We all sat round the radio and I was told fiercely to keep quiet, while the grown-ups listened anxiously.'

Wartime film stars—Clark Gable on the right. Most of the main feature films were American, because British studios had closed down. Children imitated the American accents of their screen heroes, and picked up American slang

The highlight of the week for millions of children was a visit to the pictures. In those days most towns had a cinema. Usually it was crowded for each performance, and there were long queues for popular films.

Many films had a war theme, as their titles suggest—*Target for Tonight*, *In which we Serve*, *One of our Aircraft is Missing*. But there were also coloured spectaculars such as *Gone With The Wind* or lavish American musicals for those who wanted to forget the war.

When they were sitting back in the cosy darkness of the picture house, involved in the exploits of film stars such as John Wayne or Clark Gable, people forgot all about the real war-time world outside. Even when the cinema manager announced that an air-raid warning had sounded, most of the audience, like this boy, did not leave the cinema:

'I never once left the pictures when the siren went. Very few people did. We were prepared to risk being blown up rather than miss seeing the end of the film.'

19 Travel

This poster would be familiar to any child who travelled by train during the war. It was displayed on all stations to remind the public that they were occupying travelling space that was needed for troops. Stations were usually packed with forces on the move.

The trains generally ran to time, even when an air-raid warning had gone. Passengers were given the choice of going into the station shelter or remaining on the train. Most remained on the train, unwilling to lose their seats. But there was a risk. Some trains were attacked by enemy aircraft and passengers had to crouch on the floor as bullets whistled past.

IS YOUR JOURNEY REALLY NECESSARY?

RAILWAY EXECUTIVE COMMITTEE

A railway station with many servicemen waiting for trains

Some buses were converted to run on gas, either pulling a trailer or with a tank on top

War brought a shortage of petrol, which led to rationing in 1942. At first every car owner had a basic ration, but eventually this was stopped. Families could no longer motor about the countryside for pleasure. Only people who had to travel by car for essential purposes, such as doctors, were allowed to do so.

In the early days of the war, people experimented with gas propulsion. Cars with strange balloon-like bags on the roof were a familiar sight in the street. This bag was full of gas which was used to drive the car in place of petrol. Unfortunately a whole bag of gas only took the car about twenty miles and then it had to be refilled. The process was so tiresome that the craze for it soon died down.

Buses often had a trailer towed behind which generated gas as the vehicle went along. Again, this method had its drawbacks, as this boy points out:

'Coming from school the bus had to go up a steep hill. When it reached the bottom we all had to get out and walk because there wasn't enough power to get it up full of passengers. It waited for us at the top and we got on again, out of breath.'

20 Holidays

Because of all the wartime difficulties and restrictions concerning travel, rationing and national security, the Government felt it would be wiser for families not to go away on holiday. They urged people to spend their holidays at home instead. To most people this was not a very exciting prospect, so local councils organised special events to attract them. They organised concerts, physical training displays, fancy dress parades and plays in the parks. Some families planned their own private events such as picnics, long walks, or bicycle rides in the country.

A few families still continued to go away, either to stay on farms where they could enjoy fresh eggs and vegetables, or to the seaside. But the sea was not much fun during the war, for there were none of the usual attractions.

"PERHAPS THIS'LL TEACH YOU TO STAY AT 'OME NEXT 'OLIDAY"

Long stretches of beach were closed to the public. Even those that were open were strewn with barbed wire and concrete blocks—a reminder of the invasion threat

21 Effects on Family Life

CARELESS TALK COSTS LIVES

The war badly affected family life. It split up families, destroyed their homes, and gave them less time to attend to each other's needs. Many people's close relatives were killed.

Evacuation separated children from their families. Though some returned home quickly, others were away for five or six years and saw their family only rarely, or not at all if they had been sent abroad. When the time came for the evacuees to return, their parents and home were strange to them and many found it difficult to settle back into their old way of life.

Children who remained at home throughout the war still suffered separations. Many fathers were in the forces and spent much of the war fighting abroad. They returned home only for brief visits, often turning up unexpectedly when they had swapped or wangled 24 hours leave. They were almost strangers to their children.

These families had come under machine-gun fire near Croydon Airport in August 1940. The fathers were away fighting

Saying good-bye to Daddy

A crêche where mothers could leave their young children while they were at work

Older brothers became uniformed heroes returning from Africa or North America bringing exotic, almost forgotten things like bananas, chewing gum and magazines, and filling the house with their comrades and tales of the war.

The postman became a very important figure in the family's life because he brought airmail letters which kept them in touch with relatives overseas. Unfortunately they were heavily censored. If father was stationed in Britain, his family would often move to be with him and live in digs.

Because fathers were away and mothers were helping in the war effort by working long hours in factories or in the volunteer services, many children were neglected. Sometimes boys and girls got completely out of hand and there was a great increase in juvenile delinquency.

Some fathers, brothers, uncles and cousins never returned home. They were killed in the fighting and buried abroad. Other relatives died in the air raids. Death was a thing children had to learn to accept.

The bombs robbed many families of their homes, reducing them to a mass of rubble and destroying all their possessions. They were forced to live a temporary sort of existence in reception centres.

But although the war disrupted family life, it raised the standard of living of many poorer families by providing full employment. With more money coming into the home the children were much better fed and clothed than before the war. Also the war brought people in general closer together. They were always ready to help each other and there was a feeling of togetherness in the face of danger. Nowadays many older people remember with great nostalgia the warm friendliness of the war years.

Home bombed. Mother dead.

22 Victory Celebrations

All through the dark days of the war people had looked forward to the moment when the black-out would end and the lights would go on again all over Britain, filling the streets with an almost forgotten brilliance. When the ending of all black-out restrictions came, it was a very exciting moment for everyone, but especially for the thousands of young children who had never seen a lighted street lamp. As dusk fell on Monday 24 April 1945 parents took their children out into the street to see the lights switch on.

A month later, on 8 May 1945, the war in Europe came to an end. Nazi Germany was defeated. That day was known as VE Day (Victory in Europe) and declared a National Holiday. Everybody planned to celebrate. Parents were determined to make it a really exciting day for the children because the war had deprived them of so many things. There were street parties, bonfires, dancing, and fancy dress parades.

'Our victory celebration,' a girl remembers, 'was a party for the whole street. The children were in fancy dress—myself in red, white, and blue, and my brother dressed as a farmer, pushing a trolley of vegetables representing 'Dig for Victory'. Many tables were joined together down the middle of the street for our tea and all the houses were decorated with flags and bunting.'

The victory celebrations included this firework display

Clearing up

The days that followed VE Day were probably an anticlimax, for there was no immediate return to prewar conditions. The shops did not immediately fill with oranges, bananas and sweets. Rationing did not in fact end until 1954. Also there was a lot of clearing up, sorting out and rebuilding to be done and that takes time. Wartime children had become adults with children of their own before they saw the last traces of war disappear.

Some More Books

FACT

Growing Up In World War Two, Kathleen Monham, Wayland 1979

Life In Wartime Britain, E R Chamberlin, Batsford 1972

How We Lived Then, Norman Longmate, Hutchinson 1971

The People's War, Angus Calder, Cape 1969 (Both excellent, detailed accounts of life during the war. Rather difficult reading, but useful for reference.)

FICTION

Carrie's War, Nina Bawden, Gollancz 1973 (The strange adventures of a brother and sister evacuated to Wales.)

Dawn of Fear, Susan Cooper, Chatto & Windus 1970 (Set in the Blitz.)

In Spite of all Terror, Hester Burton, Oxford 1968 (Experiences of a grammar school girl evacuee.)

Dolphin Crossing, Jill Paton Walsh, Macmillan 1967 (About Dunkirk.)

Fireweed, Jill Paton Walsh, Macmillan 1969 (Excellent account of the Blitz.)

We Couldn't Leave Dinah, Mary Treadgold, Cape 1941 (Activities of a pony club and a Nazi attempt at invasion.)

Going back, Penelope Lively, Heinemann 1975

The Machine Gunners, Robert Westall, Penguin 1977

Propaganda plays an important part in all wars. One feature of the 1939–1945 war was a fine series of posters commissioned by the British Government. Many of the posters in this book are among the best examples of poster art ever produced

Index

aircraft 17, 23, 49, 50, 55
air raids 16–21, 24, 44, 47, 51, 54, 60
air raid shelters 16–21, 43, 50
ARP wardens 6, 16
Air Training Corps 26
Anderson shelter 17, 18
animals 40, 41
Army Cadets 26

babies 9, 34
Baedeker raids 20
bananas 30, 59, 62
barrage balloons 7
Bath 20
baths 16, 38
billets 11, 12
bicycles 25, 50, 57
black market 38
black-out 23–24, 52
Blitz 20
bomb damage 6, 47, 50, 60
bombs 6, 7, 16, 28, 49, 60
Boy Scouts 26
bread 31
Bristol 20
buses 6, 56

camouflage 6
Canterbury 20
cars 23, 24, 56
Chamberlain 5
Children's Hour 52
Children's Overseas Reception Board 14
cinema 8, 52–54
clothes 12, 35–37, 60
clothes rationing 34, 35–37
Cogs 27
coupons 34, 35
Coventry 20, 22
cricket 51

'Dig for Victory' 39–41, 61
Dunkirk 44

evacuation 10–15, 42, 58

films 52, 54
First World War 5, 8, 16
fish 30, 31
food 25, 28–32, 39
food rationing 28–33, 34
football 51
France 21, 25

gardening 39–41
gas masks 8–9, 10
Germans 21, 25
Germany 5, 16, 61
Girl Guides 26
Girls' Training Corps 26

Heinkel 50
Hitler 5, 20
holidays 57
Home Guard 25, 26
Hull 20
Hurricane 50

invasion 25, 46

Junker 50

knitting 27, 37, 46

Liverpool 20
London 19, 20, 21
Lynn, Vera 53

'Make do and Mend' 35, 36, 45

meat 29, 31, 34
mending 36, 37, 45
Messerschmitt 50
Morrison shelter 18

pets 47

radio 5, 52–54
railway stations 25
ration books 29, 32
RAF 7
RSPCA 40, 47

schools 8, 10, 22, 27, 39, 42–46
Sea Cadets 26
sea-evacuation 14–15
shops 6, 28, 29, 31
sirens 16, 17, 47
Spitfire 50
sport 51
surface shelter 19
sweets 33, 62

teachers 8, 10, 13, 42, 43, 46
toys 48–49, 50
trains 6, 55
travelling 10–11, 55–6
tube stations 19

Uncle Mac 52

V1 and V2 21
VE Day 61

Wellington bomber 50
windows 6, 23
Women's Junior Air Corps 26